THIS BOOK IS
FOR THE BIRDS

P. Brian Machanic

Enjoy!

P. Brian Machanic

11-23-'13

This Book Is For The Birds has been designed to extol the beauty, diversity, and unique traits of some of the many avian species which grace the Eastern portion of the United States. Obvious constraints prevent this from being a compendium of all birds found in this area. The wildlife images displayed herein, as well as many more, can be found on Brian's website : www.natureseyestudio.com
Enjoy!

SHIRES ✺ PRESS

P.O. Box 2200
Manchester Center, VT 05255
www.northshire.com

THIS BOOK IS FOR THE BIRDS ©2013 P. Brian Machanic
Photography ©P. Brian Machanic
ISBN: 978-1-60571-198-0

Dedication

This book is dedicated to Johanna, my beloved wife of 51 years, and to our dear fledglings: Rick, Holly (Adolfi), Chris and Corey. You have nurtured me with your love, encouraged me in times of frustration, and tolerated my time away from the family while fulfilling professional obligations and pursuing extracurricular interests. You have always been my reason for being.

And now our nest is empty, but Jo and I remain invigorated by our grandchildren: Corey, Ryan and Cole Adolfi; and Olivia, Riley, Aiden, Emma, and Oakley Machanic. We are so blessed.

I'd also be grossly remiss were I not to honor my deceased parents, Philip and Evelyn (Hayes), who were always there for me and fostered my love of Nature. So too did Richard and Betty (Reynolds) Brown, my deceased in-laws, whom I cherished. God bless.

Let's Have A Look

Table of Contents

Preface

In the United States, it is estimated that there are at least some 50 - 60 million people who are self-admitted birders or bird watchers. Birders are those whose affliction for monitoring things avian is all consumptive, leading to forays afield at ungodly hours, while being viciously attacked by the biting insects which birds are supposed to eat, but obviously disdain. It is the inveterate birders who will vigorously debate whether the Flycatcher that they are looking at a mile away with their Galilean telescopes is a Willow or an Alder specie. The same dedicated group can identify the trill of a Yellow Warbler several hundreds of yards away, while all I can hear is the croaking of frogs in the marsh I'm trying to slog across.

I'm more of a bird-watcher sort, which means that I enjoy sleeping in once a month, and stop looking for nighthawks when the thunder and lightning starts. I have only a couple of well-worn bird field guides, the second of which was purchased when I thought I'd lost the first. I lack any notebooks for recording the number and species of birds seen per trip, per season, per year or per life. Such temperance has allowed my family to maintain a semblance of stability. What the neighbors don't know won't hurt. For me, F.O.Y. means Free Of Yard-work, not a First Of the Year bird sighting. My one major hang-up is an insatiable penchant for spending hours and hours at a time in a blind (a.k.a. a structure which allows the photographer to think that he / she is undetectable to feathered critters, while the "unsuspecting" subjects know full well that we are there!). The Holy Grail is that one-in-a-million shot that will someday catapult me into the Bird Watchers' Hall of Fame and allow me to generously dip into the multi-billion dollar industry devoted to supplying every imaginable need of the birding world. Meanwhile, I labor for less than minimum wage and eat a lot of fast food.

Two Benefits From Buying This Book

─────

(1) To give the author an obscene profit, which might allow him to retire and terminate such silly monologs.

(2) To further your appreciation of nature and the avian kingdom - and that's REALLY what this book is all about.

Introduction

This book is devoted to some of the more popular birds found in the Eastern portion of the United States. Even in this relatively small segment of the world, there are several hundred species of birds to be found - some being year-around residents, while others simply breed in this region, or make transient appearances therein. Some birds rank high in popularity, based on such factors as colorfulness, elegance, and / or cute habits. Cardinals, grosbeaks, orioles, buntings and bluebirds are well recognized as being very colorful - primarily the males of these species. Hummingbirds are dainty and beautiful. Chickadees, nuthatches and house wrens are cute, albeit frenetic. Much effort is devoted to feeding and / or nesting such birds in order to keep them visible. On the other hand, such birds as crows, ravens, grackles, turkey buzzards and cormorants often generate little interest - sort of the avian equivalents of Rodney Dangerfield. Hundreds of tons of bird seed, suet and nectar find their way to backyard feeders annually, but how many folks put out carcasses to feed the carrion eaters? It's discriminatory!

This is not to overlook other bird species which can do well - or better - without man's help. These include waterfowl, alcids, loons, wading and shore birds, and raptors, as well as a plethora of insectivores (i.e. insect-munchers). These are no less fun to observe than the backyard-visiting clans, but require that the observer separate himself / herself from the couch and bay window, and become the intrepid outdoor adventurer.

Even professional sports franchises seem infatuated with birds. Witness the Baltimore Orioles, the Toronto Bluejays, the St. Louis Cardinals and Arizona Cardinals, the Philadelphia Eagles, the Pittsburg Penguins, the Baltimore Ravens, the Atlanta Falcons and, yes, even the Seattle Seahawks to name a few. Moreover, irate fans of any team - with or without an avian logo - may give their rivals "the bird" at any time. What a legacy!

Well, I've Made It This Far!

Prologue

What you label another page when you've already got an introduction!

Since this book is directed to the birding fraternity, it is only fair that we further identify the two species of this austere group - i.e. birders and bird watchers. On the premise that a picture is worth a thousand words, these two mugshots may help reduce any lingering confusion as to which category you or an acquaintance may fall into. Only the police numbers have been deleted to protect the identity of the "model".

Specie: Birdericus

Specie: Bird Watchericus

American Goldfinch

Each Spring, as the earth revitalizes and a new avian breeding season dawns, the male Goldfinch undergoes a dramatic make-over, via a total molt. The drab grayish brown winter plumage is shed, and a bright yellow bird emerges, with a black cap, and black and white wings and tail. From pauper to prince. So attractive is its appearance that three states - Iowa, Washington and New Jersey - have adopted the American Goldfinch as their state bird.

The Goldfinch is found at some time of the year in all contiguous 48 states. It's a gregarious little bird, which flocks together until nesting occurs. Preferred terrain includes weedy fields, open woodland and orchards. They are feeder-friendly, munching contentedly on millet and sunflower seeds, and happy to come back for refills.

American White Pelican

The American White Pelican has been labeled by taxonomists as Pelicanus erythrorynchos, Well, at least they got the pelican genus correct! Erythrorynchos is from the ancient Greek for red-billed. Only problem is that this pelican has an orange bill! This discrepancy might not be as obvious were it not for the fact that the pelican's bill is huge. And, speaking of bills, the White Pelican also has a further embellishment on its bill during the breeding season - a flattened horn on its upper mandible. Hence, anatomic verification that this pelican does get horny during the breeding season.

What's the similarity between Humpback whales and White Pelicans? Well ... both on occasion seek their prey through teamwork, the Humpbacks rising up from below while blowing a myriad of bubbles to confuse their prey, while the White Pelicans may team up to chase their prey into shallows and corral them. The coup de grace then being the gulping in of their quarry in both cases.

Trivia

The White Pelican is content to fish while paddling on the surface, while the Brown Pelican feeds by making aerial dives on its intended prey. And now you know the rest of the story.

American Woodcock

This chunky little bird, also called a "timberdoodle" is one of the iconic upland game birds in North America. Found in states east of the Rocky Mountains, the Woodcock inhabits moist woodlands, where it can use its long bill with a flexible tip to probe the soft soil in search of worms and other invertebrates. Rather reclusive and well camouflaged, Woodcock are often not seen until they are flushed. Their rapid twisting flight makes them a challenge for bird hunters, even with a pointing dog. Woodcock-hunting aficionados yearn to encounter a "flight" of these migratory birds, as they head southward in response to crisp autumn nights in October and November.

The warmth of early Spring triggers an elaborate courtship ritual in which the male Woodcock makes spiraling flights to attract a mate. Typically, the little guy seeks out a small clearing a few minutes after sunset and again as dawn is breaking. He announces his presence with frequent "peents" and then spirals upward for several hundreds of feet. As he ascends, the wind passing through his wing primaries makes a musical twitter. At the apogee of his flight, the male then tucks his wings and plummets downward, braking on occasion until he lands at the original launch site. This whole scenario is repeated several times as the waning light is lost to total darkness, or until dawn's light intensifies.

Once mating has been consummated, the female Woodcock creates a makeshift ground nest and lays up to four eggs therein. During the ensuing incubation, this normally shy bird is remarkably tolerant of a human's presence. I've inadvertently been within 4 - 5 feet of a nesting woodcock without the bird flushing.

Once the hatching is completed, mom and her brood leave the nest site within the next few hours. The hatchlings remain on the ground for another two weeks, until their wing primaries have developed enough to allow them to fly short distances.

Atlantic Puffin

Oh, for the life of a mariner ... with a touch of Ringling Bros. just for variety. The Atlantic Puffin is a pelagic bird, spending all of its time at sea except when on shore-leave during breeding season. With its large and garish bill, eyelid "makeup", bright orange legs and feet, black and white face and body, and waddling gait, the Puffin is also labelled the "clown of the sea". Simply stated, they're cute little fellows.

When ashore, puffins aggregate in colonies and nest in individual burrows. They tend to return to the same burrow year after year. Iceland is the epicenter of breeding for the Atlantic Puffin. However, some 40% of this specie nest farther south, some on islands off the northern coast of Maine.

Only one egg is laid yearly per breeding pair of Puffins. After a prolonged incubation of some 40 days, a precocious chick is borne. The little one is able to stand immediately, and its eyes are open at birth. Nourished by a diet rich in such goodies as herring, sand eels and capelin, the nestling remains in the burrow for about six weeks. Not wanting to be a land-lubber, the young one then casts off to sea in the dark of night. Heave-ho, and bon voyage!

Tip

Check out Machias Seal Island off the coast of Jonesport, Maine as a great place to view Atlantic Puffin up close during their nesting season.

Bald Eagle

It was in the late 1770's, and the United States was a new sovereign nation - "independent, with liberty and justice for all". Our founding fathers had crafted our Declaration of Independence from Great Britain, after the strife and sacrifice of the Revolutionary War. A search was underway for a National Emblem - something that would incarcerate the "power and authority" and majesty of our new country - a symbol of freedom and our continued resolve to oppose tyranny. Story has it that in some of the battles for our independence, bald eagles were awakened from their roosts by the shouts and gunfire of the battles raging beneath them. These majestic birds were seen to circle over the battlefields, reportedly screaming as if to encourage our troops.

In 1787, the Bald Eagle was selected as our National Emblem. Its regal image is now found on many forms of our currency, as well as on the Great Seal of the United States and other patriotic printings. Interestingly, Ben Franklin and a few of his colleagues opposed this selection, arguing that the Eagle was "lazy" since it occasionally stole prey from other raptors (cleptoparasitism). How ironic that such proclivities do nothing more than mimic our current national government's lassitude and expressed willingness to tax its minions in order to promote its own agenda. Now it is our government's conduct that demeans our National Emblem. May the Bald Eagle once again rise above the fray and scream for "liberty and justice for all".

Black-capped Chickadee

Measuring about 5 inches, or less, from the tip of its bill to the tip of its tail, this busy little bird is small in stature in the avian realm, but certainly not lacking for energy. A year-around resident of the Eastern and Central states, this perky and friendly little fellow is a favorite of many bird lovers. To observe these Chickadees at a feeding station is a study of motion, as they waste little time grabbing a single seed, then flying to a nearby perch where the seed is consumed by numerous pecks. Then a quick wipe of the bill and it's back to the feeding station for a reenactment.

There's little difference in the physical appearance of the male and female of this species, but gender recognition poses no apparent problem for the birds themselves - and that's what really counts.

Burrowing Owl

Most self-respecting owls roost and nest in trees - or at least barn rafters - but not the cute, feisty Burrowing Owls. They're the blue collar clan of the owl kingdom. These little critters prefer to get down and dirty in underground burrows. They may claim squatters' rights on the abandoned dwellings of burrowing animals such as skunks and prairie dogs, although these owls are very capable of doing their own excavation. Evolution has given Burrowing Owls legs that are disproportionately long compared to their short bodies. All the better to dig with!

As true of other owl species, the Burrowing Owls hunt primarily at night, but they're also active in early daylight and in evening hours. This makes them more photographable than their strictly nocturnal brethren, as does also the relatively open terrain that burrowing owls frequent.

Found in Florida and several Western states, Burrowing Owls are threatened by the continuing development of prairie land and other open spaces where they home.

Cedar Waxwing

It wouldn't be Fall without the arrival of large flocks of Cedar Waxwings, which use fruiting trees as fast food stops during their southward migration. Replete with their black masks, these little "bandits" snatch ripened fruits, as well as red cedar cones, in a feeding orgy. They gulp down large quantities of small fruits, adroitly plucking the morsels from the stems and even catching some in mid-air. If the fruit is starting to ferment, the waxwings can get an avian high in the process!

The waxwing's name derives from the red, candle wax-like spots present on the tips of its secondary wing feathers. This marking is shared by both the Cedar and Bohemian species.

Common Loon

What could be more hauntingly beautiful than the yodels and howls of the Common Loon? In the judgement of many, the loon is one of the creatures whose presence is most synonymous with true wilderness. Right up there with the likes of wolves and moose. Moreover, the cries of the loon have been heard by some form of creatures for thousands of millennia. In France, a loon fossil has been discovered that dates back 20 million years!

The Common Loon, along with the four other loon species in North America, has both benefitted and been challenged by evolution. The loon's legs emerge far back on its belly, similar to those of another strong swimmer, the penguin. However, the penguin has mastered the talent of upright walking, while the loon staggers and stumbles while trying to walk with its body still in the horizontal plane. Indeed, it is said that this is how the loon got its name ... from walking sort of ... well, loony. The tradeoff, however, is that the rear leg placement enables the loon to be a propulsive underwater ballerina, capable of pursuing the fish it preys on to a depth of 200 feet!

Loons nest on the shores of lakes, ponds and natural islands. The proximity to the water line makes their nests vulnerable to the destruction of flooding. Their propagation has been aided by man-made nesting islands, which float on the surface, thus avoiding the devastating effect of rising water.

A typical loon nest cradles 1 - 3 eggs, with the usual brood being one or two chicks. For approximately the first two weeks of their lives, these downy, gray offspring are very buoyant and unable to dive. The youngsters tire easily and often hitch a ride on mom or dad's back. Hence, the classic picture of one or more of the chicks being transported by the dutiful parent.

Common Yellowthroat

One of the many warblers found in North America, the Common Yellowthroat has a wide range of distribution, which extends from Mexico to southern Canada. Cold weather prompts these little fellows to head for the southern part of their range during the winter months.

The Common Yellowthroat has an affinity for thick vegetation, being found primarily in marshes and other moist terrain with dense shrubs. There they dine on indigenous insects and spiders.

The male Yellowthroat is more brightly colored than the female, with an olive back, yellow throat and belly, and black facial mask. The female has more muted colors and lacks the black face mask of the male. Interestingly, the females seem more attracted to those males with a relatively large face mask. These avian ladies go for Zorro!

Dark-eyed Junco

Despite being advertised as year-around residents in the Northeastern U.S., the Dark-eyed Junco is far more prevalent in our area during the winter months. This would indicate that we're seeing Juncos that breed in northern Canada and then migrate here to winter. The male Juncos which we see annually have a dark gray or black hood, with similar coloration of their back, wings and tail. Their lower breast and outer tail feathers are white. Mild sexual dimorphism is displayed, with the darker color of the male being a more brownish-gray in the female. There are other color variants of the Dark-eyed Junco in the more western parts of our country.

Much like the Mourning Dove, the Dark-eyed Junco is primarily a ground feeder. Its penchant for terra firma is also evidenced by its tendency to nest on the ground. Despite its proclivity to keep its feet soiled, the Junco can be enticed to make slight ventures upward if the food is at that level. Hence, this picture of a Junco "tending" a mini-sleigh. Giddy-UP!

Eastern Bluebird

Of the North American songbirds, arguably the Eastern Bluebird has been accorded more idolatry than other member of this beloved group. Witness the "bluebird of happiness", or the lovely day that's a "bluebird day". Surely the charisma associated with this specie comes from their lovely colors - the adult males sporting the signature deep blue color above, with a chestnut breast and a white belly; while the female is predominantly gray above, with some light blue showing in its wing primaries and tail feathers - lovely in a more subdued sense.

Bluebirds are both good parents and (usually) devoted partners, with bonding often persisting for several years. Not to say there's no occasional philandering, however! Both parents are active in feeding the nestlings, with a diet largely of insects, spiders and grubs. Watching the nestlings scarf down this wiggling cuisine does not stoke one's appetite.

Bluebirds often have 2 - 3 broods during the Spring and Summer months. Watching a pair go through two nesting cycles this year, I was impressed with the female's ability to adapt. Her first nest of woven grass was about 2 inches deep, in a nest box whose entry was another 3 inches above this level. Resultantly, mom and dad had to do a lot of flexing in feeding their new hatchlings. The second time around, mom built a nest to within one inch of the entrance portal, and then slowly removed some of the grass as the nestlings grew. Housekeeping is definitely a learning curve!

Eastern Bobolink

Spending a good bit of my youth in Vermont farmland, I became accustomed to hearing the bubbly song of the Bobolinks as they returned to their breeding fields each May. Perched upon fenceposts or shrubs, the males would sing a melody that farmers interpreted as "bob-o-link, bob-o-link, spink, spank, spink ... plant potatoes, plant potatoes, you lazy devil, you". Pretty sassy for this 7 inch long bird that sports a "reversed tuxedo" plumage of black face and under-parts, yellowish white nape, black and gray mantle, and white rump. Only during the mating season is the male Bobolink so attired. By late summer, he begins molting to the bland brown color of his female counterpart.

Regrettably, the Bobolink population has waned over the past few decades. Many of its breeding fields in the northern tier of states and in southern Canada have been decimated by developers, grazed down by cattle, or hayed earlier in the season due to improved farm machinery. These changes have either limited Bobolink mating or destroyed their ground nests before the newborn are fledged.

Should fledging be successful. the young have but a few weeks to further mature before the start of an epic migration, carrying them some 9000 miles southward to their winter range in Brazil and Argentina. Here today - gone tomorrow!

Eastern Wild Turkey

A book on wild birds could be deemed incomplete without a little turkey talk. Wild Turkeys played an important role as a source of sustenance both for Native Americans (who in some tribes venerated this bird by incorporating its feathers in various adornments) and by the Puritans. So enamored with the Wild Turkey was Ben Franklin that he suggested that it be our country's National Bird.

Wild Turkeys have made a remarkable comeback in the U.S. over the past 60 years, rising from a population of around 30,000 to a current estimated census of 7 million or more. The catalyst for this resurgence has been the National Wild Turkey Federation (NWTF) in conjunction with state Fish and Game departments.

There are five subspecies of Wild Turkey in the U.S., the Eastern strain being one. The other subspecies include the Merriam, Rio Grande, Osceola and Gould strains.

Turkeys have an interesting social life. First, they have a diverse vocabulary, replete with yelps, purrs, putts, cutts, cackles, kee-kees, and ... of course, the tom's gobble. Secondly, turkeys are gregarious, with the hens flocking together throughout the year except when nesting in the Spring. They're joined by the toms during the breeding season, and by their poults after the hatching. Once the adult toms have done their thing, they leave to form "bachelor groups" as the hens head to nest. The bachelor groups persist for the remainder of the year, although they may merge again with the hens and poults if an abundant food source is discovered. Then its back to the boys' club. Thirdly, turkeys of both genders have a definite peck order, which, in the case of the toms, can turn downright nasty at times, with wing flailing, snood pulling, and spur lashings. Boys will be boys!

Evening Grosbeak

If one were to make an analogy between the coloration of certain birds and popular movements in the world of art, the Evening Grosbeak could be an Impressionist creation, while its rose-breasted cousin would be more Art Deco. This is not to belittle the male Evening Grosbeak, whose relatively soft browns and yellows are both attractive and remarkably harmonious with its wooded environment.

Yearly fluctuations in Evening Grosbeak sightings has proven enigmatic, but may simply relate to cyclic variations in food supply for this specie in different locales. During the breeding season, Evening Grosbeaks tend to be in isolated pairs, while in the Fall and Winter, they flock together and are easier to spot. Favored food items include spruce bud worms and box elder seeds. A scattering of migrating Evening Grosbeaks may appear at our feeders in late April, and an occasional flock of 20 - 30 may arrive in November, as they move southward. We sometimes go several years between backyard sightings, making these infrequent visitations particularly special.

Golden-winged Warbler

Over 30 species of warblers are found in the Northeastern states during the breeding season. The adult males of many of these species are quite attractive - the Prothonotary, the Blue-winged, the Blackburnian, the Northern Parula - and the list goes on. Not to be excluded from such distinction is the male Golden-winged Warbler. Its black mask and throat patch, white facial pattern, and yellow crown make this a handsome bird. Interestingly, its name-sake wing patches are more of a yellow than a golden color, but that's close enough by modern curriculum standards!

This warbler has experienced a declining population over the past 50 years, due in part to its tendency to hybridize with the Blue-winged Warbler, and also due to a decrease in its breeding habitat. The Golden-winged has an affinity for shrub-laden tangles, adding to the difficulty in sighting this specie. Moreover, the Golden-winged migrates to Central and South America for the winter months, making sightings by the birding fraternity feasible only if they themselves become "snow-birds".

Great Blue Heron

The Great Blue Heron is present either year-around, or at least during its breeding season, in all of our contiguous 48 states, as well as in parts of Alaska. This is the largest of the North American herons, with an height of approximately 36 - 55 inches and a wingspan of some 65 - 80 inches. Great Blues frequent both fresh and salt water habitats - any source of fish, which are its dietary mainstay. For diversity, this heron will also swallow other prey such as crustacea, reptiles, small birds and rodents. Yummee!

Great Blues nest in communal rookeries, where they construct large, shallow nests of intertwined branches. From 3 - 6 eggs are then laid, with an ensuing incubation of around 4 weeks. Then ... voila ... some ugly looking chicks are hatched over a few day period. Great Blue Herons are an exception to the generalization that all babies are born cute. These food-guzzling neonates are mostly a dingy grayish black, with prominent yellow eyes and bills that are disproportionately large for their bodies. A look that only a mother could love!

Ultimately, after fledging, the immature herons will gradually molt into handsome adults. Only their guttural, croaking call remains unappealing.

Great Egret

The Great Egret, also known as the Common Egret, has worldwide distribution in both moderate-temperate and tropical zones. Bedecked with entirely white feathers, this egret joins the much smaller Snowy Egret and the somewhat larger white variant of the Great Blue Heron as all-white species of wading birds that frequent wetlands, and the shallows of open bodies of both fresh and salt water.

The Great Egret is a slow stalker, whose diet is similar to that of the Great Blue Heron. In contrast to the Great Blue, which catches prey between the mandibles of its bill, the Great Egret spears its prey with its sharply pointed bill.

This egret has become the symbol of the National Audubon Society. Indeed, it was the Audubon Society that was instrumental in curtailing the harvesting of Great Egrets for their lovely breeding plumes, which cascade downward from their backs. This plumage was fashionable as an adornment for ladies' hats in the late 1800's. Audubon's intervention resulted in a progressive increase in this specie's population. The Great Egret is also one of the migratory waterbirds now protected by the African - Eurasian Waterbird Agreement (AEWA). The future currently bodes well for this lovely egret, if its habitat can be preserved.

Green-backed Heron

Large size doesn't guarantee success as a fisherman, but patience and ingenuity are definite assets in that regard. Witness the Green-backed Heron. Measuring only 16 - 17 inches in height, and having legs far shorter than several other heron species, the Green-back resorts to waiting patiently for its prey while standing on partially submerged logs, or on limbs overhanging water, or even on stout lilly pads. In addition, this heron has devised a baiting technique, wherein it attracts fish, frogs, or crustaceans by dropping bits of bait into the water beneath its perch. Prey eats food - prey becomes food. A simple formula!

We see Green-backed Herons in the Northeast from late April through early October. Then they're off to the warmer climes of states in the far South, particularly in coastal areas.

Green-winged Teal

Smallest of the dabbling (a.k.a. puddle) ducks, the drake Green-winged Teal in his breeding attire is, nonetheless, one of the most handsome guys on the pond. His chestnut brown head with a prominent dark green eye patch, gray back and green wing speculum make him readily identifiable.

With the exception of the breeding season, Green-wings move about in flocks. Their rapid, twisting and turning flight poses a challenge to the marksmanship of the waterfowl hunter. Teal frequent the shallow waters of ponds and marshes, where they dine on a variety of aquatic vegetation.

Despite their small size, Green-wings tend to have sizable egg clutches - at times numbering up to 14 - 16 per nest. Their hatchlings grow the fastest of any duck species, and fledge at about 6 weeks of age.

Trivia

While the hen Green-wing has mastered a muted "quack", the drake simply whistles as he does his duck things. He's cool!

House Wren

Not the prettiest bird on the block - with its brown topside and buffy underparts - the House Wren is still perky and cute. A significant part of its 4+ inch length is a nervous tail, which is often carried with an upward tilt and is prone to twitching. These busy little birds are widely distributed in our country and are quite cosmopolitan, being found in both urban and rural settings.

The House Wren is a compulsive nest builder, tending to fill a nesting box chock-full of twigs, to the point of virtually obstructing the entrance. Somehow, the hatchlings survive this obsessive trait, and its not uncommon for a House Wren to have more than one brood during the breeding season.

The kinetic nature of this little bird is evident even at fledging, when several heads may simultaneously cram the portal, and the fledglings tend to spill out like ping - pong balls from a lottery drum!

Northern Cardinal

One of the more popular songbirds, the Northern Cardinal is a favorite at backyard feeders throughout the Eastern and Central portions of our contiguous 48 states, with extension as far into the Southwest as portions of Texas, New Mexico and Arizona. The male Cardinal's black face and throat, contrasted by the red of its crest, body, wings and tail, creates the iconic image which is depicted by a multitude of artists as well as appearing as the logo for such sports teams as the St. Louis Cardinals (N.L.), the Arizona Cardinals (N.F.L.) and the Louisville Cardinals (N.C.A.A.). Pretty good for a 9 inch bird! Despite its glamor, the Cardinal is a "blue-collar" bird, toughing it out in the northern part of its range rather than migrating south during the winter months. Perhaps the colloquialism of "freezing my tail-feathers" initially referenced the Cardinal!

Northern Flicker ("Yellow-shafted")

Although a member of the woodpecker family (Picidae), the Northern Flicker spends much of its time foraging for insects and their larvae in the ground. That's not to say that they totally disdain pecking out a meal in timber, however. Also, as if to show that they haven't lost their wood-pecking talent, the Northern Flickers define their territory by bouts of loud hammering on trees - or whatever. I vividly remember a few mornings when a resident Flicker pounded away on an aluminum predator shield that was wrapped around a nest box's cedar post. At first I thought that the poor thing was sadly misdirected, but then realized the ingenuity of the bird in finding a louder sounding board. Heavy metal! Game on, Dude - and the female Flickers probably loved it.

The adult Flicker is a beautiful bird, with a heavily barred brown back, a white rump, numerous black spots on its light tan underparts, and a prominent black bib. The eastern variant, which is the "Yellow-shafted", has the male sporting a black moustachial stripe (a.k.a. mustache). In contrast the Flicker found in and to the west of the Rocky. Mts. - the "red-shafted" variant - has the male bedecked with a red mustache. The females of both variants lack the mustache, which wouldn't look very feminine, anyhow.

Northern Oriole

One of eight oriole species found in North America, and the only one glamorized as the logo of a major league team (the Baltimore Orioles), the Northern (a.k.a. Baltimore) Oriole breeds in parts of all of our contiguous 48 states. The resplendent black and orange markings of the adult male make him readily identifiable. As is also true of many other avian species, the female oriole is bereft of this vibrant coloring, making her less visible to predators while nesting. Practicality trumps vanity in Nature.

Interestingly, the Bullock's Oriole is considered the Western U.S. variant of the Northern Oriole specie, although the Bullock's has an orange face and a sizable white wing patch. Leave it to Nature to befuddle the taxonomists!

While part of its diet is insects, the Northern Oriole also has gourmet tastes, delighting to dine on oranges, apples, nectar and fruit jellies. This appetite allows us to attract orioles to our outdoor feeders and enjoy their presence.

Osprey

These large hawks, also identified as "fish hawks" or "sea hawks" (sound familiar, Seattle?), have refined their piscatorial skills to the point of making fishermen envious. It's an amazing sight to watch an Osprey plunge from the sky with its talons extended, become enveloped in a spray of water, and then labor to become airborne with its writhing catch. Sadly, on rare occasions Osprey have tackled more than they can handle, being then dragged beneath the surface and drowned. Apparently, the Osprey's talons don't release quickly if deeply embedded.

The resurgence in the Osprey population over the past few decades is an ecologic success story, attributable in part to the curtailment of certain insecticides. It's not uncommon now to see these magnificent birds soaring over both salt water and fresh water. Good news for bird watchers - bad news for the fish!

Painted Bunting

Sometimes, it's all in the name! Although a member of the cardinal family, the Painted Bunting lacks the crest and the relatively long tail that we associate with cardinals. This bunting is a shorter, stockier bird, with the mature male of the specie having a color pattern suggestive of a collision with a wet Andy Warhol painting. Witness the deep blue head and neck with red eye ring, a lime-green mantle, dark gray wings and tail, and red elsewhere. The female is much more demure, with green and yellow-green coloring that blends with the surrounding vegetation. Stoics simply refer to this disparity as sexual dimorphism.

The mature male's color pattern makes him hard to miss, but finding him can be a challenge for a New Englander. Unless it's a vagrant with a real wander-lust, the painted bunting doesn't frequent our neck of the woods. Only Florida provides both breeding and wintering areas for this specie. Other southeast coastal states have the Painted Buntings only during their breeding season. There also is a more western population that breeds in some central and southern midwest states and winters in Mexico.

So, let's see - New England has cold winters, salted roads, and expensive housing - enough to discourage any Painted Bunting. These birds do give us a convenient excuse for heading to Florida each January!

Tip

Check out the feeders at the Audubon Corkscrew Swamp Sanctuary in Collier county, Florida. These feeders offer an excellent viewing opportunity for Painteds.

Pileated Woodpecker

The largest of the known-surviving North American woodpeckers, the Pileated specie derives its name from its flamboyant red crown and crest (<L, pileus: cap). In profile, the Pileated Woodpecker has a long, slender body and a large, stout bill. Its prominent crest is oriented about 180 degrees opposite its bill, giving the bird a profile something like a pickaxe with wings!

The Pileated Woodpecker is an aggressive lumberjack that hammers out a living in dead or dying trees as well as in decomposing wood on the forest floor. Its forceful pecking can be heard from several hundred yards away, and the resultant large excavations, with piles of wood chips beneath, are a signature of its work. All this in quest of carpenter ants, termites, and the larvae of burrowing beetles.

Also known as "cock of the woods", the Pileated Woodpecker is the size of a small hen. It finds its home in forests in the eastern half of our country, as well as along the West coast and in some other inland states in the Northwest.

Roseate Spoonbill and White Ibis

Wading bird special - two for the price of one! Except for the obvious difference in shape and size, these two species do have a lot in common. Both are members of the Ibis family (Threskiornithidae). As waders, they share a common ecologic niche. Both are found in South, Central and North America. Both have long, red legs and long bills. In both species their bills are specialized: the Spoonbill's is spatulated, which allows it to be passed easily through muddy bottoms as the bird searches for aquatic food by using side to side head movements; the Ibis' long, curved bill facilitates the probing of the same soft bottoms of the shallows in quest of food. The Spoonbill and the Ibis both feed on crustaceans, aquatic insects, amphibians and small fish. And... both are basically white birds, although the Roseate Spoonbill develops some pink coloration due to the dietary intake of carotenoid pigments, which tint some of its feathers.

Actually, the odd couple is not so odd!

Rose-breasted Grosbeak

Its name being derived from the male's rose-red, inverted, triangular chevron on its upper breast, the Rose-breasted Grosbeak is a frequent summer resident in the Eastern and Central portions of the U.S. I remember this grosbeak as one of the "really pretty" birds that I saw in Vermont in my early childhood.

A members of the finch family, grosbeaks have the typical thick, triangular bill (a "gros" beak) of seed-eating birds. However, Rose-breasteds are actually omnivorous, dining also on fruits and insects. Their presence at feeders in Vermont is predictably from mid-May to early August. Debunking the derogatory colloquialism of "bird-brained", this grosbeak joins many other avian species in fleeing the Northern climes each Fall. While many homo sapiens shiver and fret during frigid winters, the Rose-breasteds luxuriate in Central and South America. Now who shows the better cerebration?

Ruby-throated Hummingbird

This little dynamo is one of my most favorite birds. Of the 16 species of hummers that either summer in our contiguous 48 states or are at least occasional or accidental visitors, only the Ruby-throat blesses those of us in the Northeast with its presence each summer.

How a bird well short of 4 inches in length and weighing less than 1/4 ounce can generate enough energy to sustain a wing-beat of 50 - 80 per second and a heart rate of up to 800 or more beats per minute while flying is truly amazing. Add to that their epic annual migration to and from Central America, during which they fly non-stop across the Gulf of Mexico, and the Ruby-throat is truly a physiologic marvel.

From a photographer's standpoint, these are wonderful little creatures, being readily attracted to sources of nectar and showing remarkable tolerance to humans' presence.

Given the Ruby-throat's remarkable physical abilities, it's surprising that more sports teams don't adopt it as their logo. Take the Boston Red Sox for example. What's attractive about a pair of sox that are red and over 100 years old? Much like the hummers, which are the only bird that can fly backwards, the Red Sox are also capable of going backwards as fast as they can go forward. The Boston Hummers .... hmm, it's worth considering!

Ruffed Grouse

The cool forest air is fragrant with the aromas of new growth. Quietude cloaks the woods in the predawn darkness. Suddenly, a crescendo of a thumping noise breaks the silence, rising rapidly in both frequency and loudness over a 6 - 7 second duration, then rapidly regressing to silence. About two minutes pass and the scenario is repeated ... and again, and again, as dawn blossoms and the sun makes its advent in the clear Spring sky.

These sounds are the drumming of a male Ruffed Grouse, as he seeks the attention of a possible mate. Ruffed Grouse, also known as partridge, are an iconic upland game bird found in the northern tier of states, as well as in both the Appalachians and the Rocky Mts. This specie derives its name from the ruff of feathers at the base of its neck. Both this ruff, and a feathered crest, are more conspicuous in the male grouse than in its female counterpart. These grouse have both reddish and gray color variants. They are well camouflaged in their wooded domain, with a beautiful feather patterning of brown, black and gray markings.

Remarkably, ornithologists have found little change in this specie over the past one million years. That's a pretty fair test of time.

Saw-whet Owl

This diminutive owl, measuring some 6.5 - 8.5 inches in height and tipping the scale at 2 - 5 ounces, is a true featherweight, even by owl standards. Although minimally larger than the elf owl, the Saw-whet is dwarfed by the Great Gray owl (27 inches) and the Great Horned owl (22 inches).

The "advertising" call of the Saw-whet is a series of single note toots, as one might make by blowing into a flute. Another source of a similar noise is said to be resultant from sharpening a saw blade on a whet stone. Hence the name, Saw-whet!

These little owls are present for at least some of the year in all contiguous 48 states, as well as in southeast Alaska. They tend to frequent coniferous forests, but can be found in mixed woods, where they're more easily spotted. Once found, the Saw-whet can be readily approached, as their protective mechanism is to remain motionless until their safety zone has been entered.

Saw-whet Owls nest and home in tree cavities. The female Saw-whet is a free spirit, tending to leave her feathered nestlings to be fed by their dad, while she finds love elsewhere and starts another brood during the same season. So much for monogamy.

Small birds feed on small things. The Saw-whet's diet consists of mice, vols, little birds and an occasional chipmunk or red squirrel. Fortunately, my jelly beans are still safe!

Snow Geese

Predictable snow storms in late October despite temperatures in the + 40 - 50 degree F. range? Such is true if these storms are huge flocks of migrating Snow Geese, whose numbers can whiten the sky or the feeding grounds which they frequent. Expansion of their dining locales from marshes and wet grasslands to grain fields has provided Snows with a huge boost in available nutrition and a catalyst to their population explosion over the past few decades.

Snow Geese breed on the barren tundra of the Arctic, where they nest on the ground in large colonies in the proximity of two predators: the Snowy Owl and the Rough-legged Hawk. This alliance by proximity creates the irony of using predators to help ward off more lethal predators, such as the Arctic Fox and the voracious Skua. In this hostile environment, the newborn goslings vacate the nest within hours of their birth, accompanied by their parents. It's another 8 - 10 weeks before the goslings are able to fly. Shortly thereafter, the family embarks on a 3,000 mile migration to their wintering grounds.

Snow Geese come in two sizes, the Greater Snow (Ht: 31+ inches; Wt: 7 - 9 lbs.) and the Lesser Snow (Ht: 25 - 30+ inches; Wt: 4.5 - 6 lbs.) The Lesser Snow migrates along the Central flyway, in contrast to the Greater Snow's Atlantic route. In addition, there are two color phases: white and blue. The white phase adults have all white feathers except for black wing tips. Blue phase adults have white heads and upper necks, with a large amount of bluish-gray body and wing color. The blue phase is much more common in the Lesser Snows than in the Greater variety.

Tree Swallow

The Tree Swallow is one of eight species of swallows that are found in this country. The swallow family - all slender, graceful birds - are aerial ballerinas, whose quick, darting flight provides the agility needed to catch flying insects.

The common name for this Swallow specie derives from the wooded terrain which it frequents and the nesting cavities therein. Likewise, the barn swallow, cliff swallow, cave swallow, and bank swallow draw their names from their associated topography. Anecdotally, the Tree Swallow has no aversion to utilizing man-made nesting boxes in lieu of tree cavities. Well, ... the nesting boxes ARE usually made of wood. Close counts! Moreover, Tree Swallow sounds more appealing than "Nest-box Swallow".

Adult Tree Swallows have a glossy, dark blue topside and white underparts that extend into a white throat and cheek patch. They have a shallow fork in their tails, in contrast to the deep tail fork of the similarly colored Bahama swallow.

Flocking together in large numbers as they begin their Fall migration to coastal states from the Carolinas to California, Tree Swallows can often be seen perched in long lines on telephone wires. This is said to be a social behavior, but perhaps they're just calling home.

Tufted Titmouse

One of three titmouse species found in the U.S., the Tufted Titmouse is the only one indigenous to the Eastern part of the country. This bird's soft gray color, large black eyes, and timid nature are similar to those features of the gray house mouse. However, their name derives from "tit" which means small and "mase", which is Old English for small bird. This redundancy suggests a really tiny bird, but titmice are actually about 2 inches longer than their cousins, the chickadees (both birds are in the family Paridae).

In contrast to the jaunty, often frenetic black-capped chickadees, tufted titmice are relatively shy and a bit reclusive. One might analogize the chickadees to a type A personality, while the titmice would be type B - but that would be anthropomorphic!

Titmice tend to remain paired throughout the year, so if one visits a feeder, its mate will often follow. Hence, be patient!

Wood Duck

Arguably, the drake Wood Duck is the most glamorous of North American waterfowl. Its breeding plumage is a potpourri of colors - chestnut brown, tan, red, blue-gray, dark green, black, and white - giving this duck a most ornate appearance. As the name indicates, these ducks are found in wooded terrain, including stream sides, swamps, beaver ponds and back-sets. They nest in tree cavities and in man-made nesting boxes. Two broods per mated pair is not uncommon during their protracted breeding season, with the average clutch consisting of 10 - 12 eggs. To complicate the parenting, some wood duck hens may lay eggs in another's nest. Indeed, upwards of 30 eggs have been found in some "Woody" nests. Sort of a parody on the nursery rhyme about the "old lady (hen Wood Duck) …. who had so many children (ducklings) she knew not what to do". Alas! No wonder that the call of the Wood Duck is a plaintive crying noise, rather than a quack.

Yellow-crowned Night Heron

What might you name a heron with a light yellow crown, that is primarily a nocturnal hunter? How about a Yellow-crowned Night Heron? Wow ... spot on! Certainly easier than naming a red and black bird a Cardinal, or a black and orange bird an Oriole.

The Yellow-crowned Night Heron is a year-around resident of the Gulf Coast states, but does drift northward after breeding, to as far away as Vermont and New Hampshire in limited numbers. A small heron (adult height of about 24 inches), the Yellow-crowned relies primarily on stalking and ambushing its prey. It will dine on insects, frogs and small fish, but has a dietary staple of such crustaceans as crabs and crayfish. Its red eyes and nocturnal habits are perhaps the avian equivalent of the "red eye special".

Before it was ruled illegal, Yellow-crowns used to be hunted for their breast meat, which was said to be very flavorful in a Cajun creole. That may be true, but onions, garlic, pepper and paprika can hide many tastes.

About The Author/Photographer

From his idyllic childhood years in rural Vermont, Brian has always had a love and passion for Nature and its wildlife. Despite academic demands leading to a Bachelor's degree with a Zoology major, a Master's degree in Human Pathology, a Doctorate in Medicine, and Board certification in Ophthalmology, Brian continued to pursue his interests as a naturalist. In 1990, Brian founded Nature's Eye Studio, which has served as a compendium for his wildlife and scenic photographic images, that have sold at retail outlets and on his website at: www.natureseyestudio.com. Brian's photography has appeared in many regional and national publications, and he has been the recipient of several awards for his images. Brian continues to reside in Vermont, but his photographic endeavors have taken him throughout the United States and in other continents, ranging from the Arctic to the Antarctic.

The End(s)